The Mirror

Also by William Cotter and published by Ginninderra Press

Poetry
The Darkness of Swans
The White Blood of Moonlight
Cloud Gazing
Refractions
Light Within the Stone
Pen Points
Of Forms and Shapes (Pocket Poets)
Of Light, Shade and Half-light

Stories
Thoughts By a Window

Play for voices
Of Baiame and a Tree That Said, 'Dig'

William Cotter

Mirror
New & Selected Poems

Mirror: New & Selected Poems
ISBN 978 1 76041 118 3
Copyright © text William Cotter 2016
Cover photo: Chris Matthews

First published in this form 2016 by
GINNINDERRA PRESS
PO Box 3461 Port Adelaide 5015 Australia
www.ginninderrapress.com.au

Contents

The Mirror	9
Of Turnips and Clouds	11
My Uncle's Home	12
Memories of a Wimmera Childhood	14
The Small Boy and the 'Roo Shoot	15
The Well	17
The Plover	18
Locomotive at Night	19
Wattles in Winter	21
A Memory Rekindled	22
Awakening	23
Jerry-built	24
On My Seventieth Birthday	26
Regret	27
Storm on Lake Victoria	28
The Morning After	30
The Patience of Women	31
The Violin	33
Walk Through an Irish Dawn	34
Exercising the Mind	36
Farewelling a Daughter	37
Song For a Bride and Groom	38
Love Song	39
Michael	40
My Magic Tree	41
Encounters	43
Boy in Sand	45
Coming by Boat	47
Ebenezer Ghosts	48

Of Red Rock and Murder	49
Molly and the Vermin-proof Fence	51
Refugee Camp	53
To the Fallen	54
'Wreckers'	55
Final Time Together	56
Night in the Golden Town	57
Salisbury Cathedral	59
Visit to Bath	60
Stonehenge	62
Ascending From Universal Studios	63
Bus Ride South on the Golden State	65
Morning Coffee	67
The Shopping List	68
The Night Walker	70
The Fencer	72
Rhyme For Old Men	73
The Space Between	74
South to the Cooper	75
Sputnik	76
The Drinker and the Pigeon	77

Call From the Land — 79

To Time, Light and Shade	81
Time and Tide	83
Villanelle	84
After the Fires	85
The Garden Beneath	86
Leadbeater's Possum	87
Sun, Wind, Dragon	88
Sturt's Desert Pea	89
Dawn Over Lake St Clair	91
Dolerite Cliffs	92

The Thylacine and the 'Dozer	94
Gibber Plain	95
Lake Eyre in Summer	96
Nullarbor Ending	97
The Pilbara	98
The Poetry of Earth and Sky	99
The Raindrop	100
Adam's Revenge	101
Goanna	103
The Spider Web	105
Birdsong	**107**
The Sparrow	109
Crow	110
Owl	111
Raven	112
Butcherbird	114
Eastern Spinebill	115
Ibises Returning	116
Kookaburra	117
Lyrebird	118
The Savvy Maggie	119
The Egret	120
All Visas Cancelled:	121
Seabird	123
The Curlews	125
Crescent Island	126
Songs For a Beachcomber	**127**
Night	129
Pre-dawn	130
Noon	131
Dusk	132

Kelp	133
Gannet	134
Oystercatchers	135
Pelicans Over Betka River	136
Silver Gulls	137
Albatross	138
The South Wind	139
A Beach Too Far	140
Cliffs	141
On the Cliff Edge	142
Rock Pools	143
Rock	144
Sand	145
Clouds	146
Light Over the Sea	147
Solitude	148
The Surfer	149
Afterword	150

The Mirror

Of Turnips and Clouds

He was a practical man, my father
And he moved confidently through the rows,
Chipping, clearing, laying bare the brown earth,
Turning each splayed top to an island
And pausing only to straighten his back
Before enforcing order on the next row.
He was, indeed, a man of the earth
And I watched with a child's admiration,
But then, with a child's restlessness,
Drawn to the blue sky
And the white, sloping clouds. Shapeless, at first,
They took on, as I watched, lightness and depth,
Edges and gullies. An airy landscape
I was sure had been fashioned just for me.
Disconcerted, I looked down and across.
But my father was almost out of sight
And the clouds, now dazzlingly persistent,
Would not release me.

Yes. He was a practical man, my father.
A man of the earth. And I sense, even
A life time later, a purpose missing
From my life. But he is gone. Long gone now
And I am held, still, by those sloping clouds
And floating landscapes I viewed as a child.

My Uncle's Home

        Apprehensive, I peer through the windscreen
And the withering years stare back.
Still the bluestone walls conniving with the hill,
The box-thorn hedge, tangled as ever.
But, now, a fence curbs all excesses.
The cottage, smaller than I remember,
Sports outward-looking paths,
Manicured gardens on watch.
From such order there must be no retreat,
Yet, when the stars creep out unobserved
And tumble briefly in torrents of rebellion,
Does a fox still yelp by the cemetery?
And does a child creep to a window,
Clutching excitement and fear
More precious than reason,
Rummaging through reefs of trees
For the glimpse of a tail, eyes coppered by the moon
And a ghost crossing the track?

        Out on the bay a cargo vessel,
Blunt as an old pencil,
Ploughs the passage forged between blocks of stone,
A work horse tamed, yet greedy for the open sea.
Smoke spills its way south,
Ink from a careless calligrapher's pen.
Heaped on the concrete shoreline,
Wood chips rain thick as krill.
Bulldozers purr, gantries, cables
Gleam in a spidery dawn.

      But somewhere, perhaps, warming itself
By a mossy, circular tank,
A tiger snake loops round the sun
And a fox, sharp-eyed and patient,
Waits for the dusk.

Memories of a Wimmera Childhood

       I recall the anaesthetising heat.
The browning fence posts and the rusting wire.
The brassy spikes of stubble. The thin bleat
Of ewes. The false creeks spiralling higher
In the plate glass sky. The ploughed, tumbled soil
A child might scuff his way through. Flat pebbles
Skimmed over water. Tractor smoke in coils,
Spun out or falling in blue-grey dribbles
And winter clouds plastering horizons.
Long pointed lightnings. Rain hammering sheds,
Red corrosive mud. Grumbling truck engines.
Bogged utes and swearing farmers scratching heads

       The tenuously peeping lines of wheat
And the sun, fuelled again with summer heat.

The Small Boy and the 'Roo Shoot

It was the sudden light that betrayed you,
That long white needle
Shot out between the back shed and the cow paddock
And pinning you there in the tussocks.

The filtered shadows of night you knew,
The whisper of fox breath,
The distant, cut short squeal of a rabbit
And the moon splaying out
Between the branches of the dead wattles.
Night was your friend.

But not this switched on fire,
This avalanche of frost
Coming dead straight towards you.
They were things you were not programmed for.
The centuries had not informed your body,
Given instructions here

And so you leaped,
Understandably,
Foolishly,
Straight up.
Frozen among the tussocks, you might have been safe,
Mistaken for a shadow,
Passed off as a ghost.
Moving like you did,
You were dead.

      I remember
The gunshot,
The injection of flame that caught you at the height of your leap,
The red fading comet of your body
As you hurtled towards the scrub
And the shouts,
The shouts of the men.

      Yes. I recall all of that.
But most, the crash,
The explosion as you cannoned into a tree,
The later sight of your skull,
Split like an egg

      And the held-in abhorrence of a small child
Swaying in the back of a truck.

The Well

    Outspoken on the rusty rim of the dawn,
Kookaburras are kick-starting the day,
Rattling out time while shadow cattle paint
Self-portraits on the grey canvas of the hills.

    Noon sees the Henty Street warriors, reluctant
To concede defeat, holding time at bay
And nursing their wounds on the bench outside the pub.
The ghost of my father props there, too, discussing
The secret business of men: cattle prices,
Football, fat lambs and the prospects for rain.

    I see the boys, too, caught unknowing
In the loops of siren laughter and swaying hips.
The girls I knew are grandmothers, spinsters
Or widows, grey and tremulous as shadows.

    The well of memory is clouded, now,
Its surface ruffled by the years.

    But our old family home,
Squat and stable on its street,
Speaks to me still,
Its coded memories safe
In the cleaner, clearer depths of the well.

    And now the kookaburras take charge again,
Straining the dusk through their bills

        And I sense the moon glowing briefly in the well.

The Plover

     It circles again, strafing the choppy stubble,
A pirouette of brown flame
Piercing the obfuscating haze of the afternoon heat.
But the boy is not deceived,
Crouched by the rusty tank that tilts and whispers
Above his head.
He laughs at the 'ach-ach' cry
Sharp as shrapnel,
Knowing the bird must land,
Overplay its hand
And reveal its eggs.

     His mind narrows,
A single ray of light
Fixing the descent, the braking quiver at the end
And the brown, perfect shape
Blurred among the stalks.

     The sun assaults his eyes.
But the hunter must never blink

     And she moves at last, cautious,
Precise as a nurse about her duty,
To cover her eggs,

     Sees too late the skinny legs crushing the debris
And the dark petals closing upon her brood.

Locomotive at Night

Recollections of a small boy upon the arrival of diesel locomotives to the Wimmera, early 1950s.

    Perverse, with spider webs, twigs
And the greying ghosts of shadows smeared upon its face,
The Wimmera frost, sharp-eyed persecutor of wheat fields,
Fence posts, mice,
Squares its shoulders to the plain,
Wrenches the moon from the tilt, the stumble of dead trees,
Fixes its round perfection with polished spikes of ice.

    Cross- legged among the cracked, disordered slates
Of the old church floor, silence colludes with the flinty air
And in the darkness below, breath mingles with breath,
Old bones, old blood with the restless tremor of the new.

    'Will it come tonight, Uncle Charlie,
    Really come tonight?'

    Moonlight seals the broken door
With a cold, prophetic sheen.

    'Oh, yeah, it'll come tonight.'

    The child stiffens, hears among broken stalks
The monster breathing,

    And now, where faith had once waged silent war
With time and mould, where all had once seemed pinned, secure,
Madness! Thunder honed to a shriek,
The triumph of metal storming upon the frost.
The train! The train is come.

    An owl starts in fear,
Yielding its ancient faith to the new.
But the child, caught between terror and joy,
Rides the crest of this fierce religion

        And God is plunging His yellow flame
Deep in that boyish heart,

            Sweeping, ploughing the wheat fields beyond
            And beyond

                And beyond.

Wattles in Winter

Today, seizing the rivulets of winter sun,
The wattles are bursting along the road.

In my childhood, before introspection had begun
And the sap of risk and danger flowed
Freely and unquestioned, these detonations of gold
Burst beneath the assaults of burrowing bees
As I climbed towards a blue paradise, cold,
But proud of the battle-inflicted scratches on my knees.

My unscrupulous adolescence dismissed as nonentities
These winter delights. The engines of my being, mastery and speed,
Swept me past, quite unmindful. Rejecting life's uncertainties,
I snatched from each day all that I felt I would need.

Perhaps, in my middle years, I wandered by,
Vaguely aware of a winter made brighter
And birds like fish swimming through gold into an evening sky,
Perhaps even sensed moments of nostalgia.

But now, with the years folding behind, I will stand,
Close and accepting, drink slowly, purposefully, of their nectar
And watch as the hook-billed ibises, fanned
And dark-tipped, rise to meet their future.

A Memory Rekindled

    I know that stop-start breath and pounding heart,
Those roller coasting thoughts lost in a young girl's smile.
I, too, have abandoned myself to ribboned perfume,
Believed I could make constant each transient joy
And run helter-skelter after moments that beckoned
And promised but could never be held.

    Gone, now, of course,
The see-sawing light and dark of my youth,
The pursuits and escapes,
The disappointments and the victories.

    But I see,
Poised on the edge of their Promised Land,
This boy, gawkily intense,
This girl, doe-eyed
And moving her hand like the prow of a boat
Through his unkempt hair
And I hear a voice, strangely soothing,
Taking me unawares.
'You were there, once,
Too,
In your time.'

Awakening

      It was not my mother's instruction
'Wood for the fire tonight'
That had catapulted me out to the wood heap,
Nor eagerness to watch her face light with approval
That would keep me there, by the hen house,
Skinny pre-adolescent that I was,
Stripped of thought
And flushed with raw, unmapped discordances.

      Oh, no! There was something darker, more compelling here.
Beyond the tree trunks, the split red wood
And the tight-lipped, wandering creek
Was my Eurydice,
My twelve-year-old Eve,
Come, ostensibly, to explore the green corridors of her
    father's apple trees.
With her dark hair loose and flowing above the breeze,
Her school uniform hiding her hips and embryonic breasts,
She was seduction and innocence
Gliding as one through patches of light and shade,
My friend, my antagonist,
Come, in reality, to smile at a distance, wave and dismiss me,

      But lingering as a smouldering flame
As I continued my task.

Jerry-built

An incident from my childhood, Coleraine Primary School,
February, 1948

The child's playground joy remains his dream on display.
The marbles glancing from the chimney are its calligraphic signs
And, on such a clean, bright day, bricks do not tremble or fall,
    do they?

In the distant, brown-rimmed paddock his father heaves bales
    of hay
And, he knows, subdued by his mother's will, the kitchen bench
    already shines.
The child's playground joy remains his dream on display

And time, in his hands, is the potter's clay,
Recess time, escape and the wheel on which he designs
And, on such a clean, bright day, bricks do not tremble or fall,
    do they?

He can imagine the tractor stuttering, a wedgie sighting its prey
And knows that the cat, annoyed by the kitchen cleaning, again
    reclines.
The child's playground joy remains his dream on display.

Around him the hopscotch girls, like mobile flowers at play,
Are forming, taking aim and leaping in talkative, restless lines.
The child's playground joy remains his dream on display.

But now, bell summoned, all must gather by the red brick
 chimney
And think of books and sums where the sun rarely shines.
The child's playground joy remains his dream on display
And, on such a clean, bright day, bricks do not tremble or fall,
 do they?

On My Seventieth Birthday

In my adolescence
Time, shade and light were fallen leaves
And I ran scattering them
And returning each day to do the same.
So why at seventy
Am I suddenly so desperate to capture them?
In my rampaging youth
That butcherbird fluted as tunefully
And cajoled his prospective lover just as eloquently
And I did not bother to stop in my tracks.
So why do I so urgently wish him success, now?

Is it regret, therefore, that I feel,
For the corners and spaces not explored,
The journeys and conversations left incomplete?
The knowledge
That the gannet will soar through cold, clean air,
That the clouds will retain their delicacy,
Suspended above the earth's rim,
That children will cartwheel along the beach as they do now,

After I am blotted out?

Is the good ship *Departing Years*
Semaphoring back that it is all part of ageing?
Or is something deeper working here,
An emerging awareness, painful but liberating,
That the raindrop, precarious there on its leaf
And ready to catapult down like a mini shooting star,
Will never seem more beautiful
Than the second it falls
And shatters the surface of that pool?

Regret

    I do not ask the great wheels of history to grind to a halt
Or the captains of time and events to negotiate some new path for me.

    Nor do I expect some alchemist to appear,
Comparable to the mythical Lady of the Lake
Who captured Arthur's sword Excalibur before it could disappear
And leave only cold ripples in the dark water.

    The past, we know, is unrecoverable.

    I cannot climb the stairs, years later
And make amends to some wronged person
When not even a shadow slides against a wall
And all substance is gone.

    I cannot catch the urn holding past thoughts
Before it shatters on the floor
And I am left
Helpless as the clouds of what might have been swirl above my head.

    One cannot unhinge the curse of hindsight
Nor can one retrace one's steps

    And I cannot stand with my parents,
Gaze back over my grey, tumultuous adolescence
Or early adulthood,
Ask them what dreams they had
And thank them,
Poor, honest, hard-working people that they were
For their persistence
And their gentle nudging of me towards my own.

Storm on Lake Victoria

       Marvellous, wild delusion.
The prisoner dances inside his head
And he is glad.
He thrusts his arm
And the paddle cleaves the mountains.
Winds bend, scour the water
And he is found.
The empty canyons belly now with cloud
And he shouts his disregard.
To plough forever
Fields furrowed with the rush of salt spray
Full in the face:
To spring in magic mimicry of mariners old
And feel imaginings battering in one's brain:
To neither stop
Nor let reality swing its watchful eye
Among such lovely solitude
And ignore despair's hard, steady throb
Riding serene beside:
To fling one's gaze
At a moving sky,
Feel the sleek tern wheel,
Defiant of the wind,
The distant chunk of sail
Careering:
Against the dully gleaming sky
Sense casuarinas
Skinny,
Groaning at the wind:

Beyond, observe the eagle
White-breasted,
Swinging supreme.
Could we but drive forever,
Take fantasies,
Hurl them open fisted,
Watch them shower and fire
With the cloud,
Plunge on
Through swirls of white and green,
Cast again our flowered dreams
And see the wind snatch them,
Draw them up,
Spread the sky with their splendour
And drown
With their lovely haunting of the chasms,
Despair
That rides serene
So close beside.

The Morning After

Portland, 1 January 2000

    So, it's pack up and move on, is it?
Goodbye to celebrations, sideshows with trousers patched,
The rockets with their scattered stems,
Profligate as flowers
Desperately beautiful,
Bursting,
Dying above the bay?

    And goodbye, as well,
To the faces, bland, expectant or flushed,
The brief, congenial touch of strangers bunched
On a century's edge, time suspended,
Toppled hard upon itself?

    Is that it?
That the momentous closure of a year?
And this, this oily smell of beer,
This shadow spent with its coat streaked,
Swept by a gouging wind,
This, the new millennium?

    Or,
Can we still, as we do every year,
Kick aside the fish-grey jetties
And the hauling, unsteady fog,

    Create a sun
And stamp it, indelibly, we hope,
On the cobalt heart of the sea?

The Patience of Women

    For a time,
Despite the grim railing round the bed,
There is a hanging on: the living to the dying,
The dying, perhaps, to the living.
The palliative scent of roses
Hangs above the stormy, creased bed
And we sit, making brief excursions into times past
Or the week ahead,
But returning, always.
The rasping collapse of my father,
The periods of silence, immutable as ice
Beneath the harsh electric eye,
Work slowly to an end
And I would escape
Or lash out, risk a final, undignified shout,
Extract from within the opiate swirling him away,
A word of reassurance,
Forgiveness for that long, male silence
Where feelings were seeds, dormant
And words pieces of broken china.
But, of course, I don't.

    We sit quietly, now,
The men confused, restless,
The women, summoned from centuries of grieving,
Patient by the bed.

I see only the patience of those women,
Firm against colliding night,
Knitting as a man dies
And, suddenly, my sister
Crooning gently his favourite songs.

       There exists no language, solid in the earth,
To describe his going,
Only the flimsiest sketch,
A face, ravaged,
His smile, brief,
And the bending nurse,
Compassionate above a corpse

He supposes once
Was his.

The Violin

      Not an expensive instrument; one bought,
I suspect, second hand, with what money
He could scrounge from his farm labourer's wage.
But it was my father's and he is dead.
So, I have brought it here to be repaired

      And it lies here, now, in its battered case,
Polished, brown-veined and patiently waiting
Snug, with its sleek rejuvenated bow.

      Now, in the musty quietness I hear,
The craftsman playing 'Danny Boy'. And I
Find myself adrift on an ocean of longing.

Years are peeled away and it's my father,
Tilted to the left, but just slightly stooped,
That I hear playing.

      Walled in by grandfather clocks, sheet music
And half-restored violas, I wonder
Why, more than half a life time later, tears
Should flow so freely. Are they for the days
Of my father, the solid bond we formed
Or for the warmth that we never quite found?
I cannot really say. Yet something firms
Midstream in my thoughts.
I know I will not play this violin.

Walk Through an Irish Dawn

    The closer warmth of my wife
And the comforting smell of sleep
Play like a tide, an echo through mist.

    There will be, I tell myself, a wind,
Rain fisting through trees,
The tired, gritty ends to a northern night.

    But I turn, in this foreign place,
To find the road dropping gently,
A woman patient by the gate.
She is old. Powdering her nose.
She seems only slightly out of sorts.
    'I have been waiting,' she says. 'Come.'

Her breath, her voice
Bear the touch, the sense of earthy things,
The wrapping, unwrapping of secret things.
    'Come.'

    My guide pauses briefly,
Picking the folds of her skirt clear of twigs,
Prising a fence from its thoughts.
In a meadow stand cattle,
Steaming gently like trains at their platforms.

    Ah! Now, there is a sound. Curled
In the hidden frame of a bird. Is it blackbird,
Linnet, lark
Decoding, coding, sending ahead
Its secret plans for the day?
But the woman will not be questioned.
    'Look.'

    In a break in the hedge stand walls,
The beauty of postcards,
The sideboard greying
We set among flowers
When we ourselves are old.
    'Look, now,' she says.

    There, where the moss had clung
Like slow-moving salve over wounds,
Gashes and broken stones,
There is rising a loaf,
Crusted, fresh,
Waiting its hour upon the grass.

    She is laughing, now,
My woman of the mist and the road,
Tossing the hair from her eyes.
She is taking the grey,
The sounds and the smells of earthy things,
She is making a path for the sun.

Exercising the Mind

    I remember them well. The ghostly sheep,
New shorn and bearing the moon on their backs.
Complete as continents and tossing heap
On heap of hay, Hereford cattle. Tracks

    Mud-filled or dry, we followed. Clouds we turned
To cruisers or canyons. Make-believe troops
Of Nazis we ambushed. Bracken we burned.
Chickens we harassed and chased from their coops.

    At a school assembly the two boys killed
By falling bricks. Time, when mother fell ill,
Spent on a bustling wheat farm, each day filled
With bristling heat and a child's voiceless will
To be home. All carefully filed away.

    But don't ask where I parked our car today.

Farewelling a Daughter

      There is, this spring morning,
The usual chatter of sparrows.
Moths are already crowding the buddleia.
Wrens are at work, stitching the day in a rush of blue,
Then unpicking it again.
As always, the scalloped camellias are bursting in reds and pinks
And the jonquils lie, gold, thoughtful and composed, in their beds.

      Yet, in the dry mutter of tyres over gravel,
The small, bobbing head peering back from the car,
I detect only the suffocation of winter,

      Winter and guilt,
Guilt for the silent years

      And regret,
Regret for the feelings stored
And now, too late, released.

Song For a Bride and Groom

You see the roughened summer ground, the spiked,
Brown stalks, the distant trees paused like travellers
Caught between dark and light, the rivulets
Of shadow. And, like us, the slow decline
Of colour in the sky, the light-veined gold
Still clinging on, the spreading grey ribbons,
And the sun, soft-edged on the horizon,
Gliding away.

Soon night will smooth the last wrinkles from the sky
And the stars will float through the Milky Way
As they always do.
But this sunset has been crafted for you,
This speck of time you now share together,

This memory.

Love Song

To feel
The fling of life
In the face

To risk
The river's rush,
Move slow my arm
And share its strength

Or lose
My sense
In the bowl of the sky,

Dream dreams
That flower and die
Then bloom again

Take joy
And gather for you
Those jewels
That scatter
In turn the sun

But most
My love,
To love
For the joy
Of loving you
Today

Michael

We come as strangers to this meeting place,
This white, hushed ward,
This cradle,
This moment.
You,
Like a tiny traveller from a distant land,
Rocking gently there
And I,
A stranger, too, on this shore
And silently looking down.
You from your world,
The new one,
The one not yet fully formed
And I from mine,
The old one,
The one full of hopes, love
And hidden fears.
I know the years will call you away
And you will ride the tides to distant lands.
But this is our meeting,
My son,
You from your world,
The new one,
I from mine,
The old one.

My Magic Tree

You might not believe in magic:
No more did I.
But, let me tell you something of trees –
One tree at least,
      My
      Magic Tree.
At six, it first appeared,
Tiny amidst the frost.
By eight,
I remember
Podgy Prosser's papers had just arrived,
It topped the lamp posts.
At dusk, when I returned,
Bells and silver thread clung all about,
Like stepping stones of light.
But, come the opal black of night,
Ah! Then it glowed and stretched forever,
More beautiful than I can tell.
But, the morning saw it gone
And I have told you all I can of
      My
      Strange
      and
      Lovely
      Magic Tree.

Encounters

Boy in Sand

    Fixed above the flames of stone,
He is more a statue,
Half finished,
Than a child.
Sweat alone,
Trickling and lost in the creek bed of his ribs,
Tells he is alive,

    Hearing, perhaps, the thunder,
Mechanically induced and bursting from the south,
The guts of the hill erupt as the bomb,
Heaved on its long, electric course, ploughs in
And seeing the wings triumphant
On the rim of the sun,
The trail of vapour dirtying the sky
Like the breath of a thief.

    But he stands, remote,
Grotesque,
Face, bleached in the scouring wind,
Eyes, keen as a ferret's,
Scanning the grit that clings to the pustules on his hands.

    Of no importance to him,
The sharp, apocalyptic fuss,
Bomb crunch,
Or the righteous, alien words.

      In the runnels of sand and stone
He has found,
Smooth as a pond,
A pocket of seeds,
Parcelled,
Stored and left
By a startled
Rat.

Coming by Boat

Yesterday is the prison, the dark poem one hopes to erase.
Waves forge ringlets of dreams along the hull.
Behind, lurk traipsing ghosts, the glint of guns, bewildered children.
Here the shearwaters spear ahead and the sun steeples.

Waves forge ringlets of dreams along the hull.
Words revealed on the deck can betray and so are stuffed below.
Here the shearwaters spear ahead and the sun steeples.
Footsteps, unused to the sea's vicissitudes, are reduced to shuffles.

Words revealed on the deck can betray and so are stuffed below.
Only the stars and the charcoal night have access to thought.
Footsteps, unused to the sea's vicissitudes, are reduced to shuffles.
The wind and sun collude, rasping even the will to survive.

Only the stars and the charcoal night have access to thought.
Keen as a knife unsheathing, a gunboat slices away the future.
The wind and sun collude, rasping even the will to survive.
Faces, bland as desiccated flowers, turn in fear.

Keen as a knife unsheathing, a gunboat slices away the future.
Behind, lurk traipsing ghosts, the glint of guns, bewildered children.
Boots ring out on the deck.
Yesterday is the prison, the dark poem one hopes to erase.

Ebenezer Ghosts

The Ebenezer Mission was established at Antwerp, Western Victoria, in 1861

    The mind shrinks, cracks in the growl of wind
At noon. Sky ripples, fixes its sheets of blue,
Shreds heat on the polished plain.
Stone bristles, powders, snaps at the shingle haze
And the smooth, unyielding crow
Prods from its throat the raucous stones of death.

    Did the Word unfold here once,
Rounding the scored and pitted heart of man?

    None but the great god, Bunjil, rides in comfort
Now, honing day to a fiercer blue,
Shredding with ease the splashes of dust,
The hissings of death from his eagle wings,
Rimming with bold, metallic gaze
The topple of roof,
The black girl's perfect, fatal arc
From lurch of cart,

    'I live. Ye shall live also'
Chipped and brave and blurred in the heat.

    Soon, soon may the darkness flow,
Wash broken, crimson walls to dusk and pink.
Then will the great god, Bunjil, surge,
Strong in his velvet sky,
Fixing with weeping eye,
The ghost of a frightened child,

    The sharp intensity of stars.

Of Red Rock and Murder

The actors and the audience are gone,
Packed up and gone.
Even the script is gone,
Torn to shreds and tossed into the wind and the sea.
No ghosts stand in the wings exacting revenge.
The moan of the sea
Is its own.

Only the gulls know the story now,
The acrobatic gulls and the terns.

They saw and heard it all.

The demonic choreography,
The bodies gleaming with sweat,
The faces pasty with hate or fear,
The bunching on the edge

And that final shove.

The black hands foolishly clutching at rock,
The sky hooks that never held
And the dark bodies
Writhing like airborne snakes,
Even the brief smear of red at the end.

Oh yes.
They saw and heard it all.

The curses,
The cut short screams,
The surf grinding its teeth,
The waves unperturbed and resuming their talk.

Oh yes.
They saw and heard it all

But birds know when mum is the word
And, collaring the upward currents of air,
They rode away
And the headland stands, now,
A stage swept clean
And free, even,
Of ghosts.

Molly and the Vermin-proof Fence

In memory of three Aboriginal girls who walked home

Against the heat and the battering surf of mirages
Grinding through the plains,
Three bodies, slender as rock daisies,
Girlish feet, black upon the dust pans.
Like knotted swarms of flies, fear
And the constant smell of sweat.

'Better for your children.
Away from the tribe.'
Voices from the bureaucratic past.
Starched collars, white hands coaxing.

By day the sun,
Bloodied like an animal round their necks.
At night the polished moon, their tears
And their dark eyes ever turning to the north.

'You do understand, I am sure. As a mother.
We can help them become like us.'
Moore River Settlement: windows with ribs of iron
Erect and pulsing in the heat: a prison
With whitewashed walls and hymns.

And with each dawn the minuscule footprints
Like beads in the sand,
Black, halting entries in some vast, purposeful ledger.
The bodies, thinner
And hope delicately parting their fears.

But they are coming home,
North on the dingo track,
North on the lizard track.

And the old woman remembers it all:
The wrenching apart,
The linking of hands,
The vermin-proof fence guiding them home,
The sixteen hundred kilometres crossed

And again the wrenching apart.

Years and the grating sands have covered their path.
The waters of the Milky Way are choked,
The helplessly heaving breasts
Stilled.

But the old woman remembers the silence,
The women's wailing,
The small hand, her hand
Moving like oil
Along the vermin-proof fence.

Refugee Camp

Here, dawn is a mockery, bringing no remedy
For the nightmares that scorn attempts at rest,
Label beliefs and hope as collateral debris
And mix the stench of unwashed bodies with the west
Flowing wind.
Tents, clearer now, cling on, as yesterday,
Dull as half-deflated balloons and already the children,
Lumped together in life's graveyard, are spreading grey,
Anonymous shadows across their desert prison.

To the Fallen

In every land red blossoms please the eye.
But fear and loss bring universal tears.
There is, for choking clouds, a common sky

And dreams are given no time to multiply.
The Tower of Babel sheds endless prayers.
In every land red blossoms please the eye.

All mothers croon a soothing lullaby
And hopes are swelling the hearts of lovers.
There is, for choking clouds, a common sky.

Young girls will strive themselves to beautify,
The boys to pass all tests before their peers.
In every land red blossoms please the eye.

Old men should have the time to clarify
And women time to savour memories.
There is, for choking clouds, a common sky.

The laughing children come to beautify
Each corner of the world, but bunch in tears.
In every land red blossoms please the eye.
There is, for choking clouds, a common sky.

'Wreckers'

Written after viewing Turner's painting *Wreckers*

      Unfettered, the sea heaved itself from the frame.
Clouds, tenacious as limpets, clung above the cliffs,
While, in the high, glimpsed wind, castle walls stood disjointed,
Torn like the doomed ship sloping its mast crazily,
Inevitably to the brutish waves.

      Closer, sharp as terriers and sickeningly intense,
Children scurried through the shallows,
Alert to every whim of surf,
Every vomit of colour from shattered crates.
Convulsed in the high wind and bleeding its dye upon the sand,
A dress lay in tatters, uncertain like a draining pulse.

      Distant, dirtying the sky with smoke,
A steamer slouched,
Venomous light transformed the living bodies,
With their malevolence, their collective greed, their Herculean will,
To a pasty grey.

      A truth more cogent, more to be feared
Than any maelstrom raked or pitched from the north.

Final Time Together

Evening, heavily draped
And the city's lights blinking.
Corners.
On the street, tight-lipped pedestrians
And leaves in tatters.
Voices in the bar.
Plastic, make-believe roses.
Chardonnay untouched.
Confession
And the price to pay.

Night in the Golden Town

Ignored in the copper day,
Time shuffles the dust from its chalky bones,
Stutters a path to eight o'clock
Then haltingly retreats.

    Three pubs yawn in response,
Mouthing of mateship and beer.
First, the Old Australian
Traces its filigree crisp and fine
As chain on an old woman's breast.
Next, where shadow rinses light to grey,
Stands the earthy, dull Exchange,
Coaxing true blue workers and their mates.
Third, and home to 'ethnics', 'bikies',
Blow-ins all,
Lies the sombre, bold Criterion.

    Music, subtle as stone
Heralds Mr Cool
Probing the street in his old FJ,
A knight in search of his maid,
Some consort, bosomed, lush
And worthy of his dreams.

    Bronzed in the centre of his flock
Leans patriarchal Paddy H.
He offers still the prophet's water bag,
Though no one stoops to drink.
Indeed, a sprawl of blacks
Trample upon his hopes,
Tumbling like chunks of coal to the light

    And so again the shamble of time,
The rub of grime from the eye,
The ripple of stars smooth
As scales on a lizard's back.

Salisbury Cathedral

    We alight from the bus,
Nudge to one side the gritty, grey blue of sky
And yield to the bleak vicissitudes of morning mist.
The cold, knee deep on Bishops' Walk,
Slouches, cuffs upturned
And the ghosts of Old Sarum hang in the ragged dawn.

    For a time,
As we thrust ourselves at the shallow fog,
One single, massive thought pursues us.
But then, as we watch,
Light comes limping among the distant clouds

    And now, all in a rush,
It is bursting upon cliffs,
Fisting the vast cathedral with acres of gold.
Walls, buttresses,
Stand whale-damp and splendid among the sudden blue.
Arches rear their perfect shapes. Gargoyles,
Fresh as fear in their appointed places,
Slough grey from their sneering jaws

    And we, plucked from ourselves,
Are set in wonder among those cliffs.
Above us the spire stretches
Taut as violin string,
Delicate as butterfly wing

    And the world stands revealed in stone,
The flush of green upon Salisbury Plain
And endless skies.

Visit to Bath

      Gardens fire the morning air
With spikes of red
And as we descend from the bus
We are warned to be wary of beggars.

      In a narrow street
Two workmen come tumbling barrels,
Brushing aside the churches, the steeples,
Even the ghosts that curl
And brood in the darkness below.
They see only the shapely office girls
Sprung like remembered rushing of blood.

      Ah, but we, travellers from a land
That crushes the very stuff of myths,
We are come
In search of a sacred pool,
The pool of Sulis Minerva.
Here, we are told, the cupped, transforming waters
Gleamed in the shadows,
Waging silent war
On the ancient curse of leprosy.

    Our guide smiles, retreats
And in shame
The fallen goddess turns her face to the darkness.
Gone are the numbered curses and coins,
The silver dreams of ancient men
Given to her in confidence.
Far from her bosom
They sit in modern glass to amuse the tourists.
Her marvellous, watery hair
She offers to thankless hands,
Uncaring lips.

    From the musty light, a movement, coughing.

    The Gorgon flares its severed head,
Probes with its lentoid eyes,

    The augur, Lucius Marcius Memor,
Glares from his place at the altar,
Plucks some ghastly heart from its bed,
Lifts high his bloodied hand,
Points us to the surface

    And there the beggar, older than Rome itself,
Stands with his dog.

Stonehenge

  Clouds break on the shouldering wind,
Stumble amidst distant trees,
Then yield to the darkening sky,
The downward drawing earth.

  A farmer blinks in the spitting rain,
Plunges his tractor through brown, grey skeins of shadow
That stumble and rise,
Then stops to unfasten a gate.
In the public car park buses purr or growl
And ahead of us a broken circle of stones lurches above the plain.

  Ah! For a moment the sun is clear,
Flaking silver from rock,
Running in streams from the pitted sandstone flanks.
Hands clutch at an iron rail,
Mystery blooms above our heads
And the mighty circle seems complete.

  But, now, the stones are in retreat,
The flushes of sunlight are gone,
Withered, tossed in fistfuls across the plain.

  Against time and wind nothing remains,
Only the pulse, the thrust of a tractor,
The memory of stones
Leaning in bitter lashings of rain.

Ascending From Universal Studios

      Oh! What a marvel.
The longest moving stairway
In the great outdoors. See how it chisels
A path to the smoking hills,
How quietly it moves,
How calmly it confronts the heat,
How cleverly cascades of silver and black
Are cushioned in walls
That swell and curve in the sky like silk.
Note, also, if you will,
The humble steps beside,
Stolid, white, steadfastly holding their place.

      Weary of worlds in collision,
Plastic terrors and tricks,
I stand on the moving stairs,
Going up at a sensible speed.

      But what are these,
These twin, dark spirits,
These girls resolved to be first
Among those hills?
One glides with an easy grace,
Patient on the slowly moving stairs.
The other, taut, determined on the steps,
Is joined to her friend
In a mad and joyous dash to the top.

On the landing they pause,
Flinging their ebony joy with a sudden smile.
But, now, it is off again for the summit.
Blouses strain and stretch,
Breasts flare, scarlet and bursting to be free,
Each breath, each thrust a flower.

    Below, King Kong retraces his steps,
Jaws runs mud through his teeth,
And E.T. vies for attention
With Earthquake, Avalanche, Stuntmen.

    But, now, they are sprawled at the top.
They are crumpled, triumphant.
Their bodies consume them.
Their smile, as we pass,
Is a hint

    Of the world we once knew.

Bus Ride South on the Golden State

    To the timid
Only the rivers of stone have meaning here,
Carved between the careless copper sky
And the smoky hills.

    Perhaps the bold
Confront the icons, the buried heart within
And have no fear, But I am more timid than most.
    'South on the Golden State'
Must be kept at a safe remove.

    Here, haze and palms permitting,
Lies the home of film star X
And there, a race track
Green as a scarf.

    And now,
Set in a circle
To delight a child, mushrooms!
Gleaming in silver
Above the San Andreas Fault.

    'But there will be
No Three Mile Island, here, my friend.
No Chernobyl here,
On the Golden State.'

Further south, in distant rows,
Ships of war rub shoulders with a city.
Helicopters plough the turmoil
Of blue and gold
To a threatening whirr of grey.
Against a post, fixed like cardboard,
A bearded tramp gives us God's blessing,
Promising to work for food.

'Been there each day for nine months.'
Comforting, that, from our guide,
And we shake our heads, stare,
Marvel at the cunning of men.

Hard by the *Star of India*
A child is begging. But where
Is he now, my guide, to keep me safe?

Here, indeed, is a tremor, a shadow
Sketched in the sultry sun.

But, soon, with our ice creams, our photos,
We are sweeping on,

Throwing together, child, tramp,
The glory of 'Stars And Stripes',
The mothball fleet,

Dumping them all at the border,
Securing for those in the north
Such prizes as glitter
And litter the Golden State.

Morning Coffee

All endearingly simple, those fingers
Veined as autumn cymbidium petals
Curled together on the coffee table,
Those heads bent forward, gently attentive
And that silence somehow transmitting in code.

Fuel, all of it, for one's imagining:
Remembrances surfacing from one's past,
Cleverly crafted words doing their best
Or lyrics and songs round glasses of wine.

But look more closely.
These aren't the hands of some young Romeo.
Nor is this the face of his Juliet.
His hands are scored, gnarled, patched by the years,
Her hair grey, her face lined like old paper
And yet they sit, comfortable together,
Separated only by the Arctic,
Pristine smoothness of the coffee table,
Needing no words, just a touching of hands.

The Shopping List

       They had no right, there, upsetting the smooth
Waters of our shopping. Some rituals
Must be seen as sacred. Crumpets for tea,
Apples (and isn't the price appalling)
Vegemite for the kids, bread and skimmed milk
And the solemn procession down the aisles
Must take precedence over the sideshow
Of domestic strife.

       A tick: each item snuggling into place.
The sigh of relief at the end. All done.

       Suffering has its place. We all know that.
But turning this corner into a stage
For the playing out of family ructions
Smacked of ostentation. Besides, it was
Quite unnerving, watching or avoiding
The teenage mother aware of nothing but
Her fear and her leaching tears. Her partner,
Stony-faced, distant as some singleted
Warrior, supremely statuesque and
The wide-eyed toddler, fearful between them.

       We did our best to ignore them, keeping
Just enough steerage to creep by. We swapped
Prices, enough to head off involvement
We hoped. Then disembarked at the checkout.

The girl's wild gestures and her now free tears,
The child, silent and fragile as a reed
And the firm indifference of the man
Were now a dumb show against the packed shelves.

   But I could not tick them off. They ran through
My brain weeks later, more disturbing than
Any print of Edvard Munch's *The Scream*.

The Night Walker

Night.
Doorway to the labyrinth of damaged men
And a few quick dollars.

Mist strangles the street lights.
Cars amble past

And she watches, predatory,

Defeated.

Light lingers round her throat and breasts,
Slithers down her body,
Dissolving
As a vehicle sidles off.

Would have stayed
When she was young.
Oh, yes. She was a drug, then.
A bird to be tamed: though they never quite did that,
Hauling themselves upon her.

Photos, she was told,
Had made her look like her mother:
The same eyes forever looking away,
The same body,
Loose as a mare's
To be ridden
And stabled.

But her mother had succumbed,
Catalogued the years of abuse by her husband
And stayed

While she had left.

Gone for a better life.

'Cold out 'ere, lovie.
'Ow much is it tonight?'

The Fencer

Crushing the last spikes of browning grass,
His ageing Bedford rattles to a halt
And, supple as a strip of rubber, his terrier erupts into the morning,
Keen to hunt down the night's lingering ribbons of scent.
As they do every morning, the fencer's aching joints wake
And he drags what he needs from the tray,
Noticing, perhaps, the perfectly placed posts marching up the hill,
The raw piles of clay at their feet
And the wedge-tailed eagle
Lumbering away from the gutted, gaping wreck of a lamb
And settling, bronze armoured, in steady flight along the river.
But he has no time to record the copper hammered sun
Sliding clear of the red gums, nor the few crystals of dew remaining.
The blue ice crowbar and the gravelly bite of the shovel,
They are his concern
And he will dig, fill, dig and fill throughout the day.
Dusk will see his posts having pushed further
And the taut, gleaming wires joining them.
He will wipe the scribbled dust and sweat from his face,
Call his dog,
Permit himself, perhaps, a grunt of satisfaction
And turn for home,
Thinking not of the night silence
And the nomadic moon turning his work to silver,
But of the need to do it all again tomorrow.

Rhyme For Old Men

And they drank and they danced
As the music played
And they laughed and they loved
As the flowers grew

And they wept and they prayed
As the bullets sprayed
And they clawed and they cursed
As the hatreds grew

And they ached and they aged
As the curtains closed
And they dribbled and they died
As the children grew

The Space Between

I am thought imprisoned in the stone,
Crusted in the yellow fire heat.
Brown hands I wait, curled,
Chipping stone on stone,
Flint streaming in the night.

Dead, dead the fire.
The curl of ashes creeps around me now.

In the Bora ground I wait.
I am the shade of old men, bearded.
Silence sits upon them here.

Gone, gone are the young.

I am the weeping sun, torch of Gnowee
Wandering the sky
Seeking her child.

The message in the cave,
Deep-etched:
I am the spirit seeking rest,
The woman wailing for her Christ,
In the tomb the shroud.
Yes, I am all of these.

The space,
I am the space
Filling the space between.

South to the Cooper

With Burke, Wills, Gray and King

While the sky and the sand weep tears of dust,
The wind, sharp as a scalpel, pares the crust
Of long-dead creeks. Preening its dream of death,
A crow mocks their reedy, faltering breath
And calls on their wasted frames to reject
The thin whisperings of life and accept

The cool opiate of oblivion.

The mud-soaked Gulf had brought delirium
And waves of success beating like a drum.

But now hook-beaked summer has tracked them down
And plucked life's last sparks from their companion,
Charlie Gray. Blistered hands will scrape a trench
And chiselling heat will skilfully flench

All living flesh. Yet, like rusty, dying
Pools still trembling in the wind, they will cling
To the last dregs of faith, drag through their brain
Pictures of the Cooper and hopes to gain
The coarse camaraderie of their mates.

But only the anthracite crow now waits,
Alert to the frayed hopes sinking away
And the result of that one day's delay.

On the rasping wind, forever patient.
It is rehearsing a dry, mock lament
That reaches a crude, out of tune amen

And ready with its drug of oblivion.

Sputnik

It slid, as brilliant as a diamond drill,
Through the labyrinth of stars, splitting past
From present. The frost, clamped on the low hill,
Held rigid all but this single dot cast
From the phantasmal to the actual
And set on course like some trained meteor,
Striking as a new thought made visible

And when, statuesque by his weathered door,
My old companion shouted, 'There it is,'
His voice, across the cold, metallic night,
Blossomed as a Word, a new Genesis,
A poised, new paradigm set to ignite
An Exodus past all the safe and known
Recorded on smoking tablets of stone.

The Drinker and the Pigeon

On the hotel roof, a pigeon puffs its chest,
Watching the day being unpacked,
The sun sidling across the street
And the drinker propped in his usual place.

There is a rhythm already in the traffic
And the drinker knows by sight most vehicles.
This truck will grate to a halt, next door, needing fuel.
That van will berth itself by the bank.
That car, and it is always clean, will reverse,
Carefully and with purpose, to its place under cover.
There are few surprises.
But sometimes he wonders about the occupants.
Where does that pretty young thing live?
Do the kids in that bus whinge about homework?
Does that businessman hide behind his paper at night?
Do any of those parading past pretend at love after dark?

And always they become shadows,
Laced together with cords of cigarette smoke
And softened by the welcome anaesthetic of red wine.

So, in silence,
Pigeon and alcoholic watch together
Another day unfold.

Call From the Land

To Time, Light and Shade

a ballade

Pre-dawn is the dream's quiet unravelling,
While the core of the grey-edged lake remains concealed.
Dawn is the day's door slowly opening.
Night's hard-rimmed hills have discarded their shield
And their close-held secrets are finally revealed.
Noon sees doubt and shadow finally succumb
And the sun's supremacy sealed.

Turn the prism: let time, light and shade work their charm.

Dusk slows the birds in their chattering, their flying.
The final strips of light are peeled
And long-fingered shadows have come intruding.
While reason and thought give way to impressions loosely held,
Perhaps anxieties never completely quelled
Or acceptance of the pink, enveloping calm,
The darkening world is slowly annealed.

Turn the prism: let time, light and shade work their charm.

Night clears away any stray, loitering pink and the stars spring,
In glittering white, across the sky. Carefully distilled,
Moonlight is a river of silver flowing
And the lake, coaxed by the breeze, is filled
With sparks, fragments hastily milled
And cast among the reeds. Visions disarm
The mind and the vestiges of thought linger on, unfulfilled.
Turn the prism: let time, light and shade work their charm.

Buoyed by hope of what the light may yield,
Or seeking in darkness some relieving balm,
Man must pause at the edge of life's uneven field,
Turn the prism, let time, light and shade work their charm.

Time and Tide

The Buccaneer Archipelago, Western Australia

Sky and sea merge.
Sunlight comes, careful to careen each rock.
Mangroves hang, limp as wet leather
And mirages tease the shrinking sand.

Sunlight comes, careful to careen each rock.
The creeping tide is copper-stained
And mirages tease the shrinking sand.
At dusk, saltwater crocodiles slouch, feigning sleep.

The creeping tide is copper stained
While ankle-deep, fishermen stand, brown as posts.
At dusk, saltwater crocodiles slouch, feigning sleep.
At night, whispering breezes come stroking.

While ankle deep, fishermen stand, brown as posts,
The creeping tide is copper-stained.
At night, whispering breezes come stroking.
The red-eyed salties yawn and slide through mud.

The creeping tide is copper-stained.
Mangrove hang, limp as wet leather
And, as the red-eyed salties yawn and slide through mud,
Sky and sea merge.

Villanelle

The heart of the country falters, out of sight.
Darkness stretches the veins on the roots of trees
And the wind combs the grieving hills at night.

Trucks and tankers come spilling their sickly light.
While diesels cough and choke their belly laugh,
The heart of the country falters, out of sight.

Through all the honey-coloured slopes, the might
Of commerce tramps, parades
And the wind combs the grieving hills at night.

At dawn sunlight swims in the silky wing of the kite,
Lifting it high on a rope of fire and
The heart of the country falters, out of sight.

Noon brings the whetted blade. No respite
For the truckie in his sweat and his spit
And the wind combs the grieving hills at night.

Roads bleed silver, bright,
Raw as untreated wounds. With dusk,
The heart of the country falters, out of sight
And the wind combs the grieving hills at night.

After the Fires

Shattered tree trunks above creeks and reeds.
Smoke-stained mountains scraping the sky.
Rosellas scrambling for charcoal-crusted seeds.
Through bare-boned gullies the high-pitched cry
Of cockatoos.

At night, and rusty as old nails, the stars.
The moon, its edges blurred,
Fixed above skeletal banksias.
The dry-throated wind heard
Moaning

And so, to dawn, with its dreadful silence,
Its punishment for our indifference.

The Garden Beneath

The sea begins to stir.
Hues of half-light hint of change
And soon, damask draped,
Dawn dances in the east.

Below, fish flash in fluid formation.
Pincered, clumsy crabs scuttle

And corals, creation's crafted masterpieces,
Colour the clear, clean waters,
Fresh, fragile as the flowers of Eden,

But reaching, even, the blue darkness of space.

Leadbeater's Possum

'I weep,' said the mountain wind,
'For the organ pipe trees –
The shining gums and the alpine ash,
For the loping, black cockatoos
And the dew-spangled dawns.

I weep, through the fumes
And the piles of stranded trunks,
For silence and the rippling cry of birds.

But most,
I weep for eyes perfect and clear as opals,
Ears fragile as hovering moths,
A body insubstantial as a single breath

And a world
That is dying,
Dying,
Dying.'

Sun, Wind, Dragon

        Chained at the base of the ochre-crusted hills,
The sun, its iron belly fuelled, peels
The rind from shrunken, desiccated trees
And arms the Mitchell grass with bloodied spears.

        Released, it brands the flesh of dunes and, wheeling,
Fingers a hail of gibbers and sparks. Rusting,
Rows of shattered spikes are teeth
With the yawning jaws in the earth beneath.

        At noon the wind comes grubbing through the day,
Its breath putty stuffed in smears of grey,
Its incoherent, rasping voice high
And haunting through the rafters of the sky.

        The marbled dragon, he survives, alone,
A coppered sprinter,
        Now a piece of stone.

Sturt's Desert Pea

Silent and persistent
Between the desiccated twigs
And the slow, red rivulets of sand,
A minuscule ballerina is dancing for herself,

Never centre stage,

But performing with exquisite care
Each step,
Each minute pirouette

And trusting the ancient choreography of her line,
The delicate threads of her roots
And the coral flame of her heart beating there,
Unafraid

And when her brown,
Forgettable kidney-shaped seeds fall and are lost,
She will close upon herself
And die.

There will be no public outcry,
No mourning.
No eulogy

And the acid sun will quickly burn away her remains.

But, beneath the silence of the ash and the red earth,
Something will stir
And, when the time is right,
A new ballerina will claim a corner of the stage
And dance
Beautifully,
Briefly
On the desert sand.

Dawn Over Lake St Clair

Predawn sees the chipped loose stars begin to blur.
The moon, stable and faultless earlier,
Now clings to the frayed edges of the sky, uncertain above the lake.
On the sharp-edged dolomite cliffs crimson lines blossom and break.
The breeze, nudged from its sleep, loops across the water.
Dew spangles and startles every crack and fissure.
Impatient for the day, rosellas burst in a flurry of scarlet ribbons

And, ready to assume control, the sun rears up, turns,

Clears in a single sweep night's debris and, arms outspread,
Commands a new Eden to rise and greet the day ahead.

Dolerite Cliffs

Cradle Mountain, April 2005

Before all that is,
Before life crawling or life treading,
Before hand and anvil,
Before all hammering and all shaping,
These were.

When the moon tilts
They are pillars of light
And at dawn
Pillars of cloud
Rising and filling the gorges.

At noon
They are diamond-tipped
And at their base
The wombat skull
And the scarlet globes of scoparia
Glow clean and wet.

Dusk
Gives the falling leaves a brief
Funereal red

And at night
You hear the mountains clearing their throat,
The moist whispers of a beginning wind
And the Morse code drip of water.

You expect
To find in the pillars of light and cloud
Time extolling the permanence of stone.

But listen.
Do you not hear the ghosts of mountains
And gone juts of rock,
Hammered and shaped
Before all hammering and all shaping,
Moaning of a time
Before all things

When they
Were?

The Thylacine and the 'Dozer

Probing the weathered warp of sassafras,
Mosses show their mini-heads of stars.
Where thylacines, perhaps, once stalked, silent as death,
Now just the mist's patched coat and shallow breath
Remain, smothering errant scraps of light
And staining the showy crests and pristine white
Of passing cockatoos. Where slid the feet of hunters, long
Since gone, now fungi, bright as Snow White's dwarves, crawl along
Decaying roots. But over there, where lurch the crazy
Horizontal
Trees, something, sharp-angled and breathing smoke, squares its shoulders, set for battle.

Gibber Plain

The blowtorch sun   blasts the blue
Metallic sky.   Spiked and sparking,
Copper gibbers   gleam and glance.
Salt bush,   silver-skinned,
Wallows in the dust.   Death drains
The bell-blue curve,   bends the spine
Of hills hung,   heaving and spent,

Parting, polishing   the bones of the past.

Lake Eyre in Summer

Only an enormous leap of faith
Could construct,
Here,
Long, purposeful skeins of birds
And brown, loose-flowing water
With its living cargo of frogs, fish and shrimps,
Or conjure the ancestral rumblings of pelicans
And the piping excitement of stilts
From this maddening silence,
This abnegation of hope,

This mockery
Preserved in the minute carcasses
Scattered along the shore
And the cavernous bills of half-buried pelicans
Stuffed with sand.

This is the empire of the sun and the salt,
Destroyer of dreams.

Nullarbor Ending

Brown like the plain below,
A wedge-tailed eagle comes in wide, cruising
Circles, alert, as always, for any careless flicker to show.
In a scribbled patch of shade, a dingo is lying,
Gaunt and hollow ribbed, its panting
Quick and controlled. But its hard, unblinking eyes
Are those of the hunter, programmed never to compromise.

Near the cliff edge there lies, like a ship half-buried,
The carcass of a kangaroo, its off-white skull grinning
From the sand. Its ribs are hoops scoured,
Pitted by the sandpaper wind; the wreck of a king
Preyed upon by pillaging,
Swarming flies and bulbous ants.
Here the smallest, the most voracious, have dominance.

As night approaches, the wind throws its jags of cold,
Stars begin to swim through the Milky Way
And a hard shelled moon watches the sea unfold,
Then licks the green and grey
Rocks. Seals glow silver as they play
Or probe the continent's eroding rim.
Only they hear in the caves the ocean's unchanging hymn.

The Pilbara

Land as tight-fisted as this cannot be nurtured or brought to heel,
So we plunder. We wrench out its heart, bore into its guts,
Spread mullock that bleeds black blood
And conjure grotesque, unstable mountains to put our toys upon.
We join A to B,
Hammer and fashion tracks that anchor mirage to mirage
And despatch our centipeding trains far out into the desert,
Instructing them to lift, carry and put down.
Our roads blister or sink into swirling waters.
Yet we insist that the marks we leave,
The metal fence posts and the sagging strands of gleaming wire
Are permanent hieroglyphs of progress.
But the wedge-tailed eagle, high up there
And combing the ruffled, early hair of the morning,
Will sail on, completely unimpressed,
The red kangaroo propped on dawn's unstable edge,
Will watch, cold-eyed and alert,
Then lazily lurch off to confront his day
And when history bundles us away,
The sun, sand and wind will rasp away our final dreams,
The bruised land will endure
And the fox and the dog, brought here for our sport,
Will maraud the emptiness.

The Poetry of Earth and Sky

Raw cloud fleeces.
Rainbows anchored east and west.
The flush of light through dark.
Trees, tangled or straight.
Pandanis dancing in a ragged patch of sun.
Leatherwoods, Myrtles and Horizontals competing for the
 bluest sky.
Cascading moss.
Button grass nodding approval of breeze and sun.

The healthy belly laugh of waterfalls.
The sniffle-snuffle of wombats.
Cries of loosely looping currawongs.
The quick piccolo of honeyeaters

And the rhythm of rain drops
Falling like crystals
From sky to earth.

The Raindrop

The poem
Is the moment living,
The caught-on-radar consciousness
Of its coming
And its going.

The raindrop falling.

The turning shadow,
Not the shadow turned.

The past
Is what catalogues, knits together,
Gives us the words, the emotional pigments we need.
But the moment is the present,
The present the poem.

Word and thought gone in the moment of coming.

It is the show of light,
Brief on the hill behind the tree.

Adam's Revenge

Careless of direction, the early mist
Fingers the debris on the forest floor.
Green and clumsy as a mantis, a truck
Lurches to a stop, spits out its grey phlegm
Of diesel smoke – and its single logger.

Like Excalibur unsheathed and ready,
The chain saw gives off sharp-edged spikes of light.
The sun pokes its nose down through the branches,
The breezes whisper their benediction,
But the logger chooses not to hear it.
All week he has passed by this tree and caught,
With brief interest, the soft light shredded,
The pockets of shade spread out at its base,
The brown untidy trunk and all the time
Knowing that this, this antique Huon pine,
Should be left untouched.
But what does he care,
Redundant as he will be come Monday?

Resentment tugs on the coiled starting rope,
But there is no response, save his swearing
And the muttering of the saw, coughing
To silence. He pulls again. The black smoke
Chudders up. The spinning blade flicks its chips
Of silver light and in a brown flurry
Assaults the tree.

Twenty years and certain redundancy
Give his arms the push and pull of pistons
And he laughs as the spewed dust and brown blood
Go channelling and oozing from the wound.

As the tree slants over, a long blue slit widens
Above. Retreating, he props and watches
The stricken pine heel further,
Groan like the hull of a torpedoed ship,
Steady briefly and then, as if resigned,
Cascade in a shower of brown and green
To the forest floor. Rigid, triumphant,
Now, the logger follows the last tremblings
And the ebbing flow of leaves and sawdust,
Cuts the engine with a quick finger flick,
Wipes away the sweat and hears the sad breeze
Somewhere far off.

Above, a dark, rough cloud has stuffed itself
In the blue space. But this he does not see.

Goanna

Cape Conran

He has yawned through the birth of continents,
Slid
Untroubled
From age to age,
Swallowed a million suns
And he is propped now at the edge of our camp park,
A blue-grey something close to the ground,
Looking out.

At first, only his head moves,
Left, right and straight ahead
While his tongue, split and intimidating as a snake's,
Tells him I am here, marooned on the veranda of our hut.

Now he is a slow, insinuating ooze of shadow

And now a steady roll and flow among the tents and vans.
There is no sound to speak of,
Just the whisper
One hears from bearings polished smooth, oiled and efficient.

I want to throw something,
Confront the Age of Dinosaurs,
See the great bulk ignite into panic
And scuttle away.

But he stops,
Yawns with contempt
And moves on,
Tractoring past the rubbish bins towards the next millennium

And, of course, I don't.

The Spider Web

What genius,
Without, compass, set square or computer,
Could design such perfection,
Creating, in this night of restless, thoughtless air,
Stars and wandering clouds,
Tracery so interconnected, so delicate,
That even a breath might destroy it?
Then, with only the moon's lantern light as guide,
Thread on every radiating line drops of dew
That glow like sparks in a trembling Catherine wheel,
More intense than the stars massed in the Milky way?

And why, from such perfection,
Should that white-winged moth struggle so fiercely to escape?
Can there be, in beauty like this,
A purpose other than to delight?

Birdsong

The Sparrow

Waitangi, New Zealand, March 2010

While the bleached, quarrelling gulls comb the sky
Or, like models, parade, showy and prim
On the beach and while the clever terns fly
And pirouette there and the bent-billed, trim
Oystercatchers come too, quick-stepping by,
His place is the spit-on-hand, rolled-up sleeves
Of the street. No soft watercolour sky
Mollycoddles him. No soft lyric grieves
For him or praises him. The albatross
And steepling gannet tease and brush aside
The winds, then, like the crafty Columbus,
Set sail for a world cloaked in mist and ride
The swells without complaint. His frontier
Must be a fence and a crumb his oyster

Crow

I come, crossing the crests, gullies,
The lost, looping lines of creeks,
The hard-edged hills and the hammered plains.

Born of the black beginnings of the world,
My song is of suffering, solitude and death.

Owl

heard one night at 'Riverview', Dergholm

High, already, above the hill,
The moon picks its path between the stars.
Cattle, clumped together on the river bank,
Stand, stolid as stumps,
While, suspicious in a scoured clearing,
A hare hovers, hunches and bounds away,
A brown ripple among the rushes.
Beneath the rusty shed roof, the stored bales blur into one
And, as the fog fingers the spiked phragmites
And red gums along the river,
From the damp darkness there comes the low, slow call of an owl,
Its repeated, predictable 'Mo-poke, mo-poke,'
Now fixed, now moving, now fixed again,

Drawing me back to a white, washed moon,
Chipped stars,
A creek, silent as a silver snake,
My child's shadow, small and insignificant in the moonlight
And, high up on a bluff,
An owl calling down into the valley,
Calling, calling to the present
And I sense, here on the veranda, as the sound dies away,
A sadness I cannot quite explain.

Raven

      Against the petulant sun
A raven, smooth as a woman's hand, comes
To perch on a branch,
Tapping the jewels of light
On the ribbon grass,
Flinging with noisy contempt its pitiless gaze
Upon shadows.

      Once, high on the castle walls of Carisbrooke,
I saw the subtleties, the absurdities of time
Derided like this,
The wings secretive, the bird standing
In fierce, cold winds,
The scimitar bill slashing criss-cross roofs of houses,
The stroking of shattered rock.

      Oh, how starkly it stands,
All of it, above this restless dusk:
The present, the future, the past
Dropped as a bitter curse from that throat.

      Charles, the imprisoned king,
He heard it,
Pacing his sickly, shadowed cell,
And the soldier on guard outside, scratching his fleas,
And the teenage girl
Offering her naked fear and her breast
To the castle lord

    And how clearly it rolls through my brain, now
In this familiar place.

    How practised, assured
Its grasping of the night

Butcherbird

Meticulous in black, grey and white
And still as the post he sits on,
He is the watcher,
Scissoring the long corridors of shade,
The shivering lines of poplars
And the dew-spiked stubble.

Now, like the arrow shot into the sunlight,
The missile dissecting the mist and falling,
Falling, silent with death,
He is the hunter.

Now, the butcher,
With his butchering knife and talons sprinkled with blood.

Now, the flautist, running up and down the scales,
Venturing into a melody he alone has the skill to accomplish,
His crescendos and diminuendos rippling out
Like silver water over the waking landscape

And now, once more, the watcher,
Patient,
Silent on his post.

Eastern Spinebill

I am the slightest frisson troubling the leaves,
The brown, black and gold
And the curving bill probing petals,
The will-o'-the-wisp,
The photo to be taken,
Gone too soon to be taken.
But a moment not to be missed.

Ibises Returning

In the distance, they are specks strung in loose, travelling Vs.
Closer, as they coast over sheds, paddocks and houses,
They are wings, curving, polished bills and black,
Forbidding monkish heads,

Straw-necked ibises
Coming down, in choreographed chaos,
To shed the warm air from their wings,
Swoop, probe each tree
Prop on skinny, stovepipe trouser legs
And, in low, cough-in-tunnel mutterings,
Warn off any would-be claimant.

Kookaburra

I don't need much to be content:
A few careless, well fed mice,
The occasional frog or worm,
A place to sit, think or philosophise

And, of course, time,
Time to harass the sun and nudge it from its bed,
Time to tell the sky when it should turn red,

And, most of all,
Time to watch the world go by,

The boobook owls and the filmy, flitting bats,
Moonlight, starlight and the silky smooth fox
At night,

And, in the daylight,
Time to laugh at the foolish antics of men.

Yes
It doesn't take much.

Lyrebird

I am the scribble of twigs,
The leaves breathing, parting, coming together again,
In the forest, the shape you thought you saw but couldn't be sure.
I am the stream talking to no one but itself,
The breeze imparting secrets to tree ferns.
Even the silver dew creeping over rock pools
And the mists experimenting with shapes among the trees.
I am the chain saw,
The camera shutter.

From the orchestra pit of the darkened forest
I am the music,

The link between the earth and sky.

The Savvy Maggie

    His beak sifts truth from lies and nods
To colleagues – left and right. Then, puffing chest,
Like any union man, he turns and prods
The Tory raven from his patch. The best
Of bankers stop to check the price of shares
And he, with Machiavellian ice, dispels
The rumoured slump in Tokyo. The city's
Pandemonium he tames and quells
The lunchtime rush with notes from Mendelssohn.
When hassled train commuters crowd and spin
On cliff top platforms, he will jettison
His pride and comb the railway garbage bin,

    Then, mustering his rich Churchillian strains,
Instruct the staff to free the peak hour trains.

The Egret

       She stitches water to sand,
A whisper of wings and white, reptilian head,
Gliding from pools of shade
And standing with a strand
Of sunlight caught in her bill.

       Galahs come in a rush,
Ibises form their rows,
Starlings sway in clumps,
Brawling in the shallow grass.

       But she waits,
Watching
The dragonflies flitting
From bank to bank
And the purple-backed boatmen etch
And scribble in the pools.

       Blink and you miss the thrust, the water
Crimped below,
The pulsing neck and swallow,
The shudder

       And the brief show of red
Where she had been.

All Visas Cancelled:

Or Starlings in Winter

No salvation for you this year, mate,
Cocky little beggar that you are.
You might have
Threaded your way through centuries of persecution,
Expecting, once more, sanctuary under my roof.
But not this year, mate. This year
All entry visas have been cancelled.

I can see you there, throttling back above our porch,
Weaving through those tattered polonia leaves
Still clinging to their blue corner of the sky.
I can even hear your claws on the guttering,
Your wings like the feathered prop
Of an enemy Messerschmitt slowing.
And there is your sneaky, snaky head
Burrowing under the eaves.
I've seen you there before, with your mates,
Season after season,
Flashed my torch between the beams,
Caught the oily glow of your wings,
Sworn
And banged the manhole down,
Claiming this would be the last.
I've tried the black foam
And the gutter guard.
But you've beaten me.
And here you are again, the first of your race
To migrate from the paddocks below,
Harbinger of mess and noise.

But this year, I will nip your endeavours in the bud.
Come laden with grass, felt, wool. I don't care.
This year a force will gather
Deep and secretive in the ocean beneath the roof.
And then,
Just as you are positioning your last bit of wool
And perching back to admire your skill,
A black tsunami will come
Storming through the metal beams,
To shatter your plans.
I will send in our cat.

No. No salvation for you this year,
Mate

Seabird

On seeing a solitary shearwater from the *Spirit of Tasmania*, Bass Strait, January 2009

Will time, wind and storm
Spare one as inconsequential as this,
One daring the curdling, ice-blue wastes of Abaddon
With only her ancestral dream,
Her cardboard wings
And a brain no bigger than a pea
To see her home?

What hope for such a one in this maelstrom,
Where the unwearying fiends stall, turn as she does
And reach out to pluck her down,
Down and deeper down,
To the suck, pull and swallow of the waves?

For one who hears only the mad choirs of the winds,
The low, anaesthetising sea moan
And the voice of defeat seeping like a drug,
Welling out and luring her aching body to its end,

What hope?

Surrender,
Little traveller
And the waves will toy with you for a while, perhaps.
Then, if they can be bothered,
They will disgorge your rotting corpse on some gravelly beach
Where the gulls will butcher what remains.

And what rewards should you succeed?
A mate, perhaps. A burrow shared.
A chick that might survive

And always, piercing the light and dark,
A voice, soft at first, but growing louder from the north,
'Now, you must do it all again.'

The Curlews

In the forest the curlews are calling,
Calling, calling,
Down through the dry topped gullies
And darker than parchment bats, calling
'Wee-wee, wee-wiff, wee-wee.'

'Do you sing of seasons or lovers?'
I ask.
'Of gaps in the heart or moist-eyed believers?'

'No, no. We sing of a world that is hardening,
Drying,
Warming.
Wee-wee, wee-wiff, wee-wee.
And we weep for a world that is dying.'

Now they are gone,
Down through the dry-topped gullies
And only an echo remains,
Calling, calling,
Fading, dying.

Crescent Island

    From its nest of reeds
And quite impervious to the vagaries of dusk,
A swan is watching our boat,
Motionless, vigilant,
With the spent
Rust-coloured water slopping gently beneath her.

    Along the shore
Patrolling oystercatchers, painted in vigorous black and white,
Are busy shaking the sun's dry tassels
From their smooth, red bills,
Never losing step.

    In the patchwork sky
A little tern fuses its wings to a white, purposeful flame,
Stands on the long, sloping wind,
Then falls in a blur upon the lake.
Water sprays with the intensity of wire,
But already she is free,
With a sliver of fruitless movement
Firm in her deadly bill.
Now, subdued, comical in her fluttering,
She settles beside her mate.
For a moment they are together,
Stationary, lovely as shells.

    But now she is away again,
A Christmas lily bursting above my head.

Songs For a Beachcomber

Night

In grim, gaunt grey, tangled
Melaleucas murmur among themselves.
Down the damp, dung-bleak rocks,
Half-light hesitates, hangs, fades
And darkness comes drifting down the cliffs,
Careening the cratered moon,
Fuelling the fire of a flagging meteor,
Sending it to a spiralling, spectacular death
And sprinkling specks of stars through the sky.

Pre-dawn

Seamless and subtle, the sea stirring.
Clustered clouds caught by the moon.
White and wet, the winking lighthouse.
Grey gliding gulls over surf.
The bantering breeze. Bent around rocks,
Leather limp kelp. Loose in pools,
Hues of half-light hinting of change
And stars slipping off, silver chipped.

Noon

Copper-coated, the cliffs are shimmering.
And between the blue, beaten sky
And the surf, the snakes of simmering air
Are rising, retreating, remastering the horizon.
Glimpsed gulls glide the corridors
Of the waves with white, wheeling terns
And, the sun, having scoured surf and rock,
Claims the coils of kelp, blanching
The suffocated, silver slivers of fish
And swinging slowly seaward, westward.

Dusk

Now graphite grey, the gulls are sliding
Down the day's drooping rim.
Stitched in scarlet, the sun sweeps
The sea, smoothes the shining crests
Of the waves, wanders the world's edge
And is gone. Glimpsed, on the gravelly shore,
A cormorant climbs a crimson rock,
Rivulets run in rings among stones
And stars, silver-cored, stir,
Blink and blossom above the cliffs.

Kelp

Once
Swaying in time to the deeper pulse of the sea
And riding the trailing skirts of the surf,
I am now the wreck of what was.

I, who gave comfort to the mermaids,
Knowing they had crossed the curving deeps of the world
In search of love,
Now lie here imprisoned in these stones,
Contorted, picked over by gulls,
Rasped by the wind
And carelessly mummified by the sun,

The wreck of what was.

Gannet

He is the orange-beaked one,
In the cloud-flecked sky, the long-winged seeker
Circling the sun,

Now, the striking, resurfacing hunter

And now, the orange-beaked one,
In the cloud-flecked sky, the long-winged seeker
Circling the sun.

Oystercatchers

They are the quick-thinking walkers,
The prim, precise in Sunday black and white ones.
The orange-stockinged ones,
The sagacious, nodding philosophers,
Setting down their wisdom in the sand
Or meditating on some prominent rock.

But, they do not welcome intruders –
The young lovers, the recalcitrant dogs,
The bent old men or the ructious children

And, if disturbed, they will flounce off,
Black cassocks flapping in the wind
And noisy in their objection.

Pelicans Over Betka River

Seen in the distance, they are insubstantial shapes
Brightening or darkening the corners and crevices of the clouds,
Merely outlines in some half-completed pastel.

But now, closer and clean in their configurations,
They are cannon bursts of black and white,
Wings and forward pointing bills

And now, settled in their flight
And closer still,
They are gliding, smooth as manta rays,
Each manoeuvre controlled by the flexing,
Never the flap, of their wings,
Each rise and fall calibrated, as if by magic,
The product of some secret concert of purpose

And now, dipping their wings in the cold, west-flowing wind,
They are Sunderland flying boats,
Dropping, skimming, bellying and settling on the water

And now, there they are, rocking gently together,
All twenty of them,
Dismissing the world with a sequence of leathery yawns.

Silver Gulls

We are, to you, the groupies,
The garrulous go-getters on the beach,
The casual, hands-in-pockets boys,
Strutting or propping on bollards or decks.

But, we are, in fact,
The Jolly Rogered set,
The snafflers of half-chewed chips,
The entrails of gutted fish,
Carelessly guarded slices of meat,
Anything, to be honest, that takes our fancy,

And never too proud to muscle in,
Push aside
And, if necessary, pinch from our mates,

But, happy to remain, for you,
The layabouts, the groupies,
The garrulous go-getters on the beach.

Albatross

I am the white flame kindled by the early sun.
The shadow teasing the broken tops of waves,
The long-winged one

Half-seen through the chaos of mist and rain,
The lonely mile after mile voyager
Glimpsed, lost and briefly found again.

The South Wind

Sometimes
I come in fits and starts,
Content to snap at the heels of the surf
And erase your children's patterns in the sand,

Sometimes, lazily, you might even say, leisurely,
The conciliator.

But sometimes,
Hell-bent on heaving breakers up the beach,
I tumble the heavy-bellied clouds one upon the other
And laugh as they bucket rain down over the shore
Or barrage the rocks with shafts of fire.

Yes, I come in many forms,
Many moods,
Always the controller.
But never controlled.

A Beach Too Far

Death of a shearwater

Yet again those detonations of the heart kick started his wings,
Catapulting him towards the blurred dusk and the beach he knew.
Bur tonight, the long praxis of flight, embedded in his genes, collapsed.
Salt spittle, foam and the white, whip-striking lightning
Fouled each calculation he made.
Ahead, far ahead, the staggered skeins of his fellows struggled on,
Disappeared into the rain
And he persisted, alone,
Propelled by a will not really his own
And an auto pilot planted in his brain.
But, finally, the storm swung him high,
Held him briefly, then threw him back, like a dark crucifix
Into the arms of the sea.

Cliffs

Against the bull-roaring, bare-knuckle surf
And the uppercutting winds,
Weathered and gnawed though we are,
We stand at the ready.
In the brief times of peace
We may gather and scatter the sun's early rays
And cushion the transition from daylight to night.
But, knowing the sea and the chiselling wind
Will turn and bite again
We are never off guard.

On the Cliff Edge

I have heard the mumbling, stumbling city
Wake to Monday's manic out of kilter
Tramp and chorus. Heard the footpaths' dirty
Gutters swilling mud and leaves together,
The morning's bandied office talk, the hissing
Machine-made coffee and the phone's hypnotic ring

And now I hear the chaos of seas storming,
Waves racing to batter and shatter on rocks,
On stilted legs, pied oystercatchers calling,

High and clear above the ocean's aftershocks,
Gulls looped round the sun, corkscrewing,
Breasting the wind and frantically squawking.

All of them welcome. All holding at bay a silence
That would summon the past
And all its ghostly itinerants.

Rock Pools

Summers and the blue, brown pulse of holidays,
Sidewinding crabs
Spidering away with their black, bulbous eyes fixed upon you,
The skittering flakes of fish you tried to catch in your hands,
The dark crevices you turned into canyons
And the secrets they held.
You remember them, don't you?
The jewels that danced beneath your feet
And the joys flung up to you with every tidal change?

Were they not the sunlit dreams you once held dear
Before the time of growing up
And hardening?
Could you not look down once more,
Even for a moment?

Rock

I bear on my face
Time's vicissitudes.
The bands of red, brown and grey
Running together in the sun
Mark my resilience,
Time's immensity
And, in it,
Your mortality.

Sand

Quality assured, I remain Time's proven parchment,
Cheap and available to all: the committed, the indolent,
The scribblers, the scribes, the sketchers
And even the sculptors.
But, be warned.
Of all your footprints, your clumsy hearts with their love notes,
Your scribblings and your sculpted, make-believe boats,
Not one will remain.
The tide and the wind will leave not even a stain.

Clouds

We are the morning's skeins unravelling
And night's forgotten words still drifting,
The stage made ready for play and dancing
And the set prepared for your children's dreaming.

We are the artists who darken the sun
And complete the shading night had begun,
The scallywags painting the moon for fun
And making sure the Milky Way must be totally redone.

We are the long-haired riders
And the grey-capped raiders,
The lightning bearers
And the drummers bringing thunder.

> At dawn, we are Time's crimson edging
> And, at dusk, day's scarlet ending.

Light Over the Sea

Dawn light
Is the promise
Tiptoeing through the trees and barely rippling the sea.

At noon,
It is the bold bronzing of the melaleucas
And a child's delight scattering the sand.

In the afternoon,
It is the undisciplined, glorious tossing of petals
Over the spiked or scalloped waves,

In the evening,
The solitary, scarlet cloud loosely held in the west,

At night,
The silent, unfolding moon
And the stars stitched in the folds of the Milky Way.

Solitude

The long, loosely looping waves
Shape the shifting shadows on the sand
And down the dull, darkened sky
A strip of sunlight slides and disappears.
High, haunting and harrowing, a sea eagle
Scours the scored sea, its wings
And head hard as hammered steel.
Clouds curtain the cliffs and somewhere,
Buried in the broken banksia clumps
A woop-wooping wonga pigeon
Woos the unthinking bushland
And feet feel the fingering surf
Coldly curling and coming again.

The Surfer

Over the patchy sand and the half-buried rocks,
He has swum, supple and smooth as a reptile.
He is far out, now, amidst the threads of foam,
The glimmering, cascading gannets and the sea's thunder.
The sinister, sloping darkness that could lure him down,
Down to perpetual sleep, brings no fear.
He is arm, muscle, shoulders,
Youth.
His is the rhythm of body, board and the sea
And, while the grey, discoloured gulls perform their crazy loops.
He turns, waiting for the sea's outstretched arm
To lift,
Gather
And sweep him shoreward.

Afterword

I have been writing for at least thirty-five years. And much of my poetry endeavours to explain, to myself, as well as to others, the relevance of my experiences. Perhaps, as we grow older, we are drawn to reflect more often on our childhood. I have done this in quite a few of the poems in this collection. As I look back over my early years, I can appreciate the sacrifices of my parents, who, in spite of having little money, encouraged me to continue my education – and, ultimately, my writing.

My own two children, Michael and Katrine, have enabled me to see more clearly the richness of childhood. I am grateful to them.

To Dr Francis Macnab, a special thanks for helping me untangle some of the difficult issues in my life. Some of these conflicts and resolutions I have explored here.

And to the friends who have enriched my life and stimulated so many ideas to explore, thanks also.

The natural world has always been of real interest to me – more particularly, the therapeutic value it can have for us all. And I would like, here, to express my thanks to my good friend, Jim Reside, with whom I have spent much time exploring the wonderful world around us.

Writing is, of necessity, an isolating experience and I am most grateful to my wife, Kay, who, for many years, has given me the freedom to enjoy my isolation, lock myself away and write. She has also been a constructive critic of my work.

Finally, a word of appreciation to my publisher, Stephen Matthews. He has encouraged my writing for many years. Without an understanding publisher, much of what we write would never surface or be read by others. This seems particularly true of poetry. So, to Ginninderra Press, many thanks.